EMMANUEL JOSEPH

Valley Visionaries and Realty Rulers, Human Stories Behind Their Business Success

Copyright © 2025 by Emmanuel Joseph

All rights reserved. No part of this publication may be reproduced, stored or transmitted in any form or by any means, electronic, mechanical, photocopying, recording, scanning, or otherwise without written permission from the publisher. It is illegal to copy this book, post it to a website, or distribute it by any other means without permission.

First edition

This book was professionally typeset on Reedsy.
Find out more at reedsy.com

Contents

1	Chapter 1	1
2	Chapter 1: The Seed of Ambition	3
3	Chapter 2: The Risk Taker's Gamble	5
4	Chapter 3: The Art of Reinvention	7
5	Chapter 4: Building Bridges, Not Walls	9
6	Chapter 5: The Visionary Mentor	11
7	Chapter 6: From Garage to Global	13
8	Chapter 7: Navigating the Storm	15
9	Chapter 8: The Power of Partnership	17
10	Chapter 9: Beyond Profit	19
11	Chapter 10: Breaking Barriers	21
12	Chapter 11: The Innovator's Dilemma	22
13	Chapter 12: The Legacy of Visionaries	23

1

Chapter 1

Introduction
In a world where success stories often dominate headlines and social media feeds, it's easy to forget the human struggles, sacrifices, and perseverance behind those achievements. The tales of business magnates and industry leaders are often portrayed as glamorous and effortless, overshadowing the hard work and resilience that paved the way for their triumphs. This book, **"Valley Visionaries and Realty Rulers: Human Stories Behind Their Business Success"**, aims to peel back the layers of these success stories and uncover the deeply personal journeys that define them.

At its core, this book is about people—ordinary individuals with extraordinary dreams. Each chapter delves into the life of a visionary who dared to dream big and took bold steps to turn those dreams into reality. These are not just stories of financial success and business acumen, but of human spirit, courage, and determination. They are stories that resonate with the universal pursuit of purpose and fulfillment, transcending the confines of the business world.

Through the lives of Olivia, Ahmed, Maria, Rahul, Clara, Mark, Jason, Javier, Lisa, Tom, Hannah, and Kwame, we explore a diverse array of experiences and backgrounds. From the rural fields of Kansas to the bustling streets of Lagos and the innovation hubs of Silicon Valley, their journeys are as varied as the landscapes they navigate. Yet, despite their different paths, they share a common thread: an unwavering commitment to their vision and an indomitable spirit that drives them forward.

This book also highlights the importance of resilience and adaptability in the face of challenges. Each story is a testament to the fact that success is rarely a straight line. It is often marked by setbacks, failures, and moments of doubt. But it is through these trials that the true essence of a visionary emerges. The ability to learn from failure, adapt to changing circumstances, and persist despite the odds is what sets these individuals apart and propels them toward greatness.

Moreover, **"Valley Visionaries and Realty Rulers"** underscores the impact of mentorship, diversity, and inclusivity in the world of business. The stories of Clara's dedication to mentoring young women, Kwame's efforts to break down racial barriers, and Hannah's commitment to ethical entrepreneurship demonstrate that success is not just about personal gain, but about lifting others and creating a positive impact on society. These visionaries understand that true success is measured not only by financial achievements but by the lasting legacy they leave behind.

As you journey through the pages of this book, you will be inspired by the tenacity, creativity, and passion of these remarkable individuals. Their stories serve as a reminder that behind every successful business is a human story—a story of dreams, struggles, and triumphs. They invite you to reflect on your own aspirations, embrace the challenges along the way, and believe in the power of your vision. Welcome to **"Valley Visionaries and Realty Rulers"**—a celebration of the human spirit behind business success.

2

Chapter 1: The Seed of Ambition

In the hushed stillness of rural Kansas, a young girl named Olivia Dreamer stared out over the endless fields of wheat, her mind a whirlwind of grand possibilities. The daughter of a modest farmer, Olivia's childhood was punctuated by the rhythmic hum of tractors and the golden sway of crops in the wind. But her heart beat to the tune of a different song—one filled with innovation, transformation, and endless curiosity.

One warm summer evening, as Olivia and her father sat on the porch watching the sunset, he handed her a worn-out book about the world's greatest inventors. "Olivia," he said, "you can be anything you want. The world is much bigger than this farm." Those words, simple yet powerful, planted a seed in her heart. Olivia's eyes twinkled with a newfound determination. She knew she was destined for something beyond the familiar confines of her family's farm. The journey of a thousand miles had begun with a single step.

Years later, Olivia found herself in the pulsating heart of Silicon Valley. The energy of the place was intoxicating—a bustling hub of creativity, ambition, and relentless pursuit of dreams. She embraced it with open arms, diving headfirst into the world of technology. Surrounded by like-minded visionaries, she felt a kinship she had never experienced before. Her journey was just beginning, and the seed of ambition that had been planted years ago was starting to grow into something magnificent.

But the path to success was not a straight line. Olivia faced countless challenges and setbacks. The industry was competitive, and there were times when she doubted her abilities. Yet, every failure was a lesson, every obstacle an opportunity. She persevered, driven by the promise she had made to herself and the vision that had taken root in her heart. The late nights, the moments of self-doubt, the sacrifices—they were all part of the journey.

As Olivia's startup began to gain traction, she became a beacon of hope for others who felt like outsiders in the tech world. She shared her story freely, inspiring countless young dreamers to pursue their passions. She made it her mission to create a culture of inclusivity and support, knowing firsthand the power of encouragement and belief. And as her company grew, so did the impact of her work, touching lives and shaping the future of technology.

3

Chapter 2: The Risk Taker's Gamble

Ahmed had always been the kind of person who thrived on challenges. Growing up in Lagos, Nigeria, he was known for his keen intellect and unwavering determination. After graduating from university, he landed a high-paying job at a prestigious multinational company. The stability and financial security were more than most could hope for, but Ahmed felt a gnawing restlessness. He yearned for something more—a venture that would allow him to leave his mark on the world.

One evening, while discussing his aspirations with his close friend Samuel, Ahmed confessed his dream of starting his own real estate company. Samuel, always the pragmatic one, cautioned him about the risks. "You have a stable job, Ahmed. Why gamble it all away?" But Ahmed's mind was made up. He believed in his vision and was willing to take the leap, despite the uncertainties that lay ahead.

With his savings and a small loan from his family, Ahmed founded **Amani Realty**. The initial days were tough—navigating the complex world of real estate, building a client base, and managing finances. There were moments when he questioned his decision, especially during the sleepless nights and endless days of hard work. But the challenges only fueled his resolve. He knew that success was a result of perseverance, and he was determined to see his vision through.

Gradually, Amani Realty began to gain traction. Ahmed's innovative approach to real estate—emphasizing transparency, customer service, and ethical practices—set his company apart from the competition. Clients appreciated his honesty and dedication, and word of mouth spread quickly. His reputation grew, and so did his business. The risks he had taken were paying off, but Ahmed remained grounded, always striving to improve and expand his services.

Years later, Amani Realty had become one of the leading real estate firms in Lagos. Ahmed's journey from a secure corporate job to a successful entrepreneur was a testament to the power of vision and courage. He had not only achieved financial success but had also created jobs and opportunities for others. His story inspired many young Nigerians to pursue their dreams, reminding them that sometimes, taking a risk is the first step towards realizing one's true potential.

4

Chapter 3: The Art of Reinvention

Maria was an artist at heart, with a passion for painting and sculpture. Growing up in a small town in Spain, her days were filled with creativity and imagination. But as she entered adulthood, she found it increasingly difficult to make a living solely from her art. Financial pressures and societal expectations pushed her to consider alternative career paths. It was a challenging time, but Maria was determined to find a way to channel her creativity into a sustainable profession.

Her breakthrough came during a trip to Barcelona, where she was captivated by the city's stunning architecture. The intricate designs, the harmonious blend of old and new, and the innovative use of space sparked an idea. What if she could combine her artistic talents with architectural design? With newfound clarity, Maria enrolled in an architecture program, immersing herself in the study of structural engineering and design principles.

The transition was not easy. Maria had to adapt to a new way of thinking, balancing creativity with technical precision. But her perseverance paid off. Her unique perspective as an artist allowed her to approach architecture with fresh ideas and innovative solutions. She began designing cutting-edge buildings that blended aesthetics with functionality, earning accolades and recognition in the industry.

Maria's journey of reinvention was a testament to the power of adaptability and resilience. By embracing change and leveraging her strengths, she transformed her career and created a niche for herself in the world of architecture. Her story resonated with many, inspiring others to explore new paths and reinvent themselves in the face of challenges. Maria had proven that it was never too late to pursue one's passions and that the art of reinvention was a powerful tool for personal and professional growth.

5

Chapter 4: Building Bridges, Not Walls

Rahul grew up in a bustling neighborhood in Mumbai, India. The crowded streets, vibrant markets, and close-knit community shaped his early years. But as he grew older, he became increasingly aware of the stark disparities in housing and living conditions. While some lived in luxury, many others struggled with inadequate housing and poor infrastructure. This disparity troubled Rahul, igniting a passion for social change.

With a background in engineering, Rahul saw an opportunity to make a difference through technology. He founded **Shelter Solutions**, a company dedicated to creating affordable housing solutions for underserved communities. His approach was simple yet revolutionary—leveraging technology to design cost-effective, sustainable, and scalable housing units. By partnering with local governments and NGOs, Rahul's company was able to implement these solutions in various parts of the city.

The impact of Shelter Solutions was profound. Families who had lived in substandard conditions for years finally had access to safe, comfortable homes. Rahul's work not only improved living standards but also fostered a sense of dignity and hope among the residents. His commitment to building bridges, rather than walls, resonated deeply with the community and inspired others to join the cause.

Rahul's story was a powerful reminder of the potential of technology to drive social equity. By combining his technical skills with a passion for social change, he had created a lasting impact on the lives of countless individuals. His journey underscored the importance of using one's talents and resources to give back to society and create a more just and equitable world.

6

Chapter 5: The Visionary Mentor

Clara had always been a trailblazer. As one of the few women in her tech company, she had faced her share of challenges and biases. But Clara was undeterred. Her journey to the top was marked by resilience, determination, and a commitment to excellence. She rose through the ranks, eventually becoming the CEO of a successful tech firm. But Clara's story was not just about her personal achievements—it was about the countless lives she touched along the way.

Recognizing the barriers that women often faced in the tech industry, Clara made it her mission to mentor and support young women entering the field. She established **Women in Tech**, an organization dedicated to empowering women through mentorship, networking, and professional development. Clara's vision was to create a more inclusive and diverse tech landscape, where women could thrive and succeed on their terms.

Through her mentorship, Clara provided guidance, encouragement, and opportunities for young women to advance their careers. Her dedication to their growth and success was unwavering. She celebrated their achievements, learned from their challenges, and fostered a sense of community and support. Clara's legacy was not just her own success but the ripple effect of her mentorship, which empowered a new generation of women to pursue their dreams and make their mark in the tech industry.

Clara's story was a testament to the power of mentorship and the importance of giving back. By lifting others as she climbed, she had created a lasting impact that extended far beyond her own career. Her journey inspired countless women to believe in themselves, strive for excellence, and break down the barriers that stood in their way.

7

Chapter 6: From Garage to Global

It all began in a small garage in Palo Alto, California. Mark and Jason were college friends with a shared passion for technology and innovation. They spent countless hours tinkering with computers, writing code, and dreaming up ideas for their startup. Their modest beginnings were fueled by a relentless drive to create something revolutionary—a product that would change the way people interacted with technology.

With limited resources and a shoestring budget, Mark and Jason poured their hearts and souls into their project. They faced numerous challenges, from technical glitches to financial constraints, but their determination never wavered. They believed in their vision and were willing to put in the hard work to make it a reality.

Their breakthrough came when they developed a groundbreaking software that revolutionized data management. The product quickly gained traction, attracting the attention of investors and industry leaders. What started as a small garage operation soon evolved into a thriving tech company, with offices around the world and a diverse team of talented individuals.

Mark and Jason's journey from garage to global success was a classic Silicon Valley story. Their innovative spirit, combined with their relentless pursuit of excellence, had propelled them to new heights. Their company became a beacon of innovation, inspiring countless other entrepreneurs to pursue their dreams and push the boundaries of what was possible.

The story of Mark and Jason was a powerful reminder of the potential of entrepreneurship and the transformative power of technology. Their journey demonstrated that with passion, perseverance, and a willingness to take risks, anyone could turn their dreams into reality and leave a lasting impact on the world.

8

Chapter 7: Navigating the Storm

Javier's success in the real estate market seemed almost unstoppable. From a young age, he had a keen eye for valuable properties and a natural talent for negotiation. By his early thirties, his real estate business in Miami had grown into a flourishing empire. But as the global economic downturn loomed, Javier faced a storm unlike any he had encountered before.

The recession hit hard, and the once-booming real estate market came crashing down. Property values plummeted, and investors became wary. Javier's company, which had been on an upward trajectory, suddenly found itself on the brink of collapse. The financial strain was immense, and the pressure to keep the business afloat was overwhelming.

But Javier was not one to back down from a challenge. Drawing on his resourcefulness and strategic thinking, he devised a plan to weather the storm. He made difficult decisions, cutting costs, renegotiating deals, and focusing on the core strengths of his business. It was a period of intense hardship, but Javier's resilience and determination never wavered.

Slowly but surely, his efforts began to pay off. As the economy started to recover, Javier's company emerged stronger and more agile. He had not only survived the downturn but had also positioned his business for future growth. The experience had taught him valuable lessons in adaptability, perseverance, and the importance of staying true to one's vision, even in the face of adversity.

Javier's story of navigating the storm became a source of inspiration for many. It was a testament to the power of resilience and the ability to turn challenges into opportunities. His journey reminded others that success was not just about the highs but also about how one handled the lows.

9

Chapter 8: The Power of Partnership

Lisa and Tom's paths crossed at a tech conference in San Francisco. Both were passionate about innovation and had complementary skills—Lisa was a brilliant programmer, while Tom excelled in business strategy and marketing. They quickly realized that their combined talents had the potential to create something extraordinary.

After several brainstorming sessions, they decided to co-found a tech startup that focused on developing cutting-edge software solutions for small businesses. The partnership was a perfect blend of creativity and practicality. Lisa's technical expertise allowed them to build robust and innovative products, while Tom's business acumen ensured that their solutions reached the right audience and generated revenue.

Their startup faced its fair share of challenges, from securing funding to navigating the competitive market. But Lisa and Tom's mutual respect and shared vision kept them motivated. They worked tirelessly, often burning the midnight oil to meet deadlines and refine their products. Their complementary skills and unwavering support for each other were the foundation of their success.

As their startup grew, it became evident that the power of partnership was a key driver of their achievements. Lisa and Tom's collaboration created a culture of trust, innovation, and shared responsibility. Their company not only thrived but also became a model for other startups, demonstrating the importance of finding the right partner and working together towards a common goal.

Lisa and Tom's story highlighted the strength of collaboration and the impact of combining diverse talents. Their journey was a reminder that success often comes from working together and leveraging each other's strengths to overcome challenges and achieve greatness.

10

Chapter 9: Beyond Profit

Hannah had always been passionate about social justice and environmental sustainability. After completing her studies in environmental science, she knew she wanted to make a positive impact on the world. But she also understood that traditional business practices often prioritized profit over people and the planet.

Determined to challenge this mindset, Hannah founded **EcoSolutions**, a social enterprise that focused on developing sustainable products and practices. Her business model was built on the concept of the triple bottom line: people, planet, and profit. She believed that a successful business could be both profitable and socially responsible.

EcoSolutions quickly gained recognition for its innovative approach to sustainability. From eco-friendly packaging to renewable energy solutions, Hannah's company was at the forefront of the green business movement. Her commitment to ethical practices and social responsibility resonated with customers, investors, and employees alike.

Hannah's journey was not without its challenges. Balancing financial sustainability with social impact required careful planning and strategic thinking. But her unwavering belief in her mission kept her going. She surrounded herself with like-minded individuals who shared her vision and were dedicated to making a difference.

As EcoSolutions grew, it became a beacon of hope for those who believed in the power of ethical entrepreneurship. Hannah's story demonstrated that businesses could thrive while also contributing to the well-being of society and the environment. Her legacy was a powerful reminder that success was not just about financial gain but also about creating a positive impact on the world.

11

Chapter 10: Breaking Barriers

Kwame had always dreamed of making a difference in the world of real estate. Growing up in a predominantly Black neighborhood in Atlanta, he was acutely aware of the systemic racism and biases that often plagued the industry. But he was determined to break down these barriers and create opportunities for others like him.

After earning his degree in real estate development, Kwame faced numerous challenges in his career. He encountered discrimination and prejudice at various stages, but his resilience and determination kept him focused on his goals. He founded **Equity Realty**, a real estate firm that prioritized diversity and inclusion.

Kwame's approach was simple yet powerful: he actively sought out and hired individuals from diverse backgrounds, provided mentorship and training, and created a supportive and inclusive work environment. His efforts paid off, and Equity Realty quickly became known for its commitment to social justice and its success in the market.

Kwame's journey was a powerful reminder of the importance of diversity and inclusion in business. By breaking down barriers and creating opportunities for underrepresented communities, he not only achieved personal success but also paved the way for others to follow. His story inspired many to challenge the status quo and strive for a more equitable and inclusive industry.

12

Chapter 11: The Innovator's Dilemma

Sophia's tech company had experienced rapid growth since its inception. As the CEO, she was proud of the innovative products and solutions her team had developed. But with success came new challenges. Sustaining innovation in a rapidly changing market required constant adaptation and a willingness to embrace change.

Sophia faced the classic innovator's dilemma: how to maintain the company's competitive edge while managing the demands of a growing business. She knew that resting on past successes was not an option. To stay ahead, her team needed to continuously push the boundaries of creativity and innovation.

She encouraged a culture of continuous learning and experimentation within the company. Her leadership style was collaborative and inclusive, valuing input from all team members and fostering an environment where new ideas could flourish. Sophia's dedication to innovation paid off, as her company continued to develop groundbreaking products that kept them ahead of the competition.

Sophia's story underscored the importance of staying agile and adaptable in the face of change. Her journey demonstrated that true innovation required a commitment to learning, a willingness to take risks, and the courage to embrace new ideas. By fostering a culture of innovation, she ensured her company's long-term success and impact.

13

Chapter 12: The Legacy of Visionaries

The final chapter ties together the common threads of these extraordinary stories, emphasizing the human element behind every business success. It celebrates the visionaries and rulers who have not only achieved remarkable success but have also inspired others to dream big and make a difference.

The legacy of these visionaries is not just about their individual achievements but also about the ripple effect of their actions. Their stories remind us that behind every successful business is a human story of passion, perseverance, and purpose. By sharing their journeys, they inspire us to pursue our dreams, overcome challenges, and create a lasting impact on the world.

As we reflect on the stories of Olivia, Ahmed, Maria, Rahul, Clara, Mark, Jason, Javier, Lisa, Tom, Hannah, and Kwame, we are reminded that the path to success is rarely a straight line. It is filled with twists and turns, highs and lows, and moments of doubt and triumph. But through it all, these visionaries have shown us that with determination, resilience, and a commitment to our values, we can achieve greatness.

Valley Visionaries and Realty Rulers: Human Stories Behind Their Business Success

In a world where success is often measured by profit margins and market shares, the true essence of achievement lies in the human stories that drive these accomplishments. **"Valley Visionaries and Realty Rulers"** takes you on an inspiring journey through the lives of twelve remarkable individuals who have left an indelible mark on the worlds of technology and real estate.

From the vast fields of rural Kansas to the bustling streets of Lagos and the innovative corridors of Silicon Valley, these visionaries come from diverse backgrounds and experiences. Yet, they share a common thread: an unwavering commitment to their dreams and an indomitable spirit that propels them forward. This book delves into the deeply personal journeys of Olivia, Ahmed, Maria, Rahul, Clara, Mark, Jason, Javier, Lisa, Tom, Hannah, and Kwame, uncovering the challenges, sacrifices, and triumphs that define their paths to success.

Through their stories, you'll explore the power of ambition, the resilience required to overcome obstacles, and the importance of adaptability in an ever-changing world. You'll witness the transformative impact of mentorship, the significance of diversity and inclusivity, and the profound effect of ethical entrepreneurship. Each chapter offers a unique perspective on what it means to be a visionary, highlighting the human element behind every business achievement.

"Valley Visionaries and Realty Rulers" is more than just a compilation of success stories; it's a celebration of the human spirit. It serves as a powerful reminder that behind every thriving business is a person with dreams, fears, and aspirations. These stories inspire readers to pursue their passions, embrace challenges, and believe in the power of their vision.

Join us on this captivating journey and discover the extraordinary stories of the visionaries who have not only achieved remarkable success but have also inspired others to dream big and make a difference. Welcome to **"Valley Visionaries and Realty Rulers: Human Stories Behind Their Business Success"**—a testament to the resilience, creativity, and passion that drive human achievement.

www.ingramcontent.com/pod-product-compliance
Lightning Source LLC
LaVergne TN
LVHW020744090526
838202LV00057BA/6228